Celebrating Akron's History in Picture Postcards

Editors: Chuck Ayers, Russ Musarra

Postcard Source: Ruth Wright Clinefelter

Published by the Summit County Historical Society
Akron, Ohio
2000

Greetings from Akron is made possible in part by a grant
from the City of Akron's 175th Celebration Fund.

Copyright © 2000, Summit County Historical Society, Akron, Ohio

SUMMIT COUNTY
HISTORICAL SOCIETY

All rights reserved. No part of this book may be reproduced in any form without written permission from the publisher.

Printed in the United States of America

Hardcover: ISBN 1-883916-06-2
Paper: ISBN 1-883916-05-4

Editors: Chuck Ayers, Russ Musarra
Postcard Source: Ruth Wright Clinefelter

Printed in Wadsworth by Merrick Graphics, Inc.
Printed on 100% Utopia I Gloss Text and 100% Utopia I Gloss Cover

Layout by Creative Keystroke & Design Services, Inc.

Summit County Historical Society
550 Copley Road
Akron, OH 44320-2938
Phone: (330) 535-1120
Fax: (330) 376-6868

CELEBRATING AKRON'S HISTORY
IN PICTURE POSTCARDS

Contents

Introduction: How this project came to be . . . . Page 6
Section 1 - Akron Before 1910 . . . . Page 9
Section 2 - 1910 to the Great Depression . . . . Page 59
Section 3 - 1930 to 1950 . . . . Page 108
Section 4 - 1950 to Present . . . . Page 120

PLEASE NOTE: *Most of the postcards have been slightly enlarged beyond their original size.*

Introduction

No one person is credited with having "invented" the picture postcard, but if Frances B. Murphey had been around 100 years ago, she could well have qualified for the honor. Miss Murphey, who died in 1998 after a newspaper career that spanned more than 50 years, was an inveterate postcard collector and well known for creating postcards from photos and other printed images she cut to the proper size and shape for mailing.

Ruth Clinefelter, whose postcards are the basis for this book, lists Miss Murphey among the people who influenced her as a collector.

"She trained me," Ruth says with a smile, recalling the time Miss Murphey made her own Akron postcard from a color photo she had taken of the city's new Canal Park baseball stadium.

Ruth has cards she got when she was four years old, but she didn't start collecting them in earnest until about 20 years ago when she saw her hometown's history depicted in vintage cards on sale at an Akron antique shop.

"I looked at those Akron cards and I was hooked," she said. "Those early cards - that was my grandfather's Akron. Until I walked into that store I didn't know you could buy old postcards."

Before that discovery Ruth had purchased post cards only when she couldn't adequately capture a scene in her own photos. Now she says, "postcards are the only vestige left of some of these places."

A case in point is Akron's South Howard Street, which was eliminated with the creation of the Cascade Plaza in the 1960s. Her brother, John Wright, also a collector, influenced her, too. His passion was South Howard Street, which today exists only in people's memories, old photographs and vintage postcards.

Ruth's collection includes scenes that represent moments in her family history. Her parents rented canoes at the Summit Lake livery and paddled on the canal to Young's Restaurant at Nesmith Lake. Vintage cards in her collection show children playing at Perkins and Union parks.

Postcards were the E-mail of the early 20th Century. Mail service was good and many people didn't have telephones, so people kept in touch with each other by postcards sent within the same city.

Early cards, such as the one shown here of Akron's Carnegie Library, carried their messages on the front. Cards with divided backs, with space for both addresses and messages, were not permitted in the United States until 1907, although the divided back was allowed earlier overseas, first in England, in 1902, then France, in 1904, and Germany in 1905. This change left the fronts of cards free for pictures or designs.

This book represents a large portion of Ruth's collection, with some cards from the personal collections of Agnes Barnett of the Summit County Historical Society Service League, Leo Walter of Stagecoach Antiques and Akron architecture expert

Jim Pahlau, as well as some from institutions, specifically the Akron Art Museum, Akron General Medical Center, the University of Akron, and for views of the Canal Park stadium, Lock 2 Park and Greater Akron, Nu-Vista Prints.

The impetus for the book is the 175th anniversary of Akron's founding as a canal town in 1825, but it is a volume for any year, filled with scenes dating from the 1850s to the present. The organization and production was a volunteer effort of a committee of the Summit County Historical Society, with support from the City of Akron's 175th Celebration Fund.

Serving on the committee, along with Ruth, were artist Chuck Ayers, Julia Gammon, University of Akron Press Marketing Director, attorney Fran McGovern, University of Akron cultural anthropologist Lynn Metzger, University of Akron archivist John Miller and writer Russ Musarra.

Postcards as we know them were brand new when this image of
Akron's Carnegie Library was sent in 1905.

This 1873 view of the Akron skyline graced a card sent in 1908.

Akron Before 1910

Akron was made for picture postcards, built as it was on the banks of the Ohio & Erie Canal in the Cuyahoga River Valley. Akron was carved out of the wilderness in 1825 because the canal – the superhighway of its era – was being dug from Lake Erie to the Ohio River.

The Little Cuyahoga, which fed the Cuyahoga River, provided water power to fuel Akron's early industries, which included milling and clay products. Akron had a second canal, the Pennsylvania & Ohio, which flowed in from the east and ran down the middle of Main Street before it joined the Ohio & Erie. It was the reason Main Street is so wide.

Akron is as historic as it is picturesque.

It is where, along the Cuyahoga River, two or three boats are said to have been built to supply Commodore Perry in the Battle of Lake Erie during the War of 1812.

It is where abolitionist John Brown raised sheep in the days before he militantly expressed his opposition to slavery. The John Brown home, now a museum operated by the Summit County Historical Society, is where Col. Simon Perkins Jr., the son of Akron's founder, and his wife, the former Grace Ingersoll Tod, lived while their stone mansion was being built across the street on a hillside just west of the town. Their home, completed in 1837, is now the Society's headquarters.

It is where Ferdinand Schumacher earned the title Cereal King of America. His company, which became Quaker Oats, began in 1856 and survived a devastating fire in 1886.

It is where Dr. Benjamin Franklin Goodrich built the first rubber plant west of the Alleghenies in 1870, beginning a manufacturing era that would make Akron the rubber capital of the world.

These and many other early Akron scenes have been preserved through the magic of photography, lithographic genius and the enterprise of postcard makers and collectors.

Some scenes in this section, such as the ruins of the Hower Building, were as timely as the day's news. A postcard bearing that photographic image was mailed within days of the fire that destroyed the building on May 18, 1909.

Other scenes present early 20th Century views of residences that were later adapted for other uses in the community, such as B.F. Goodrich president B.G. Work's home, which became the Akron Woman's City Club, and clay products executive Byron Robinson's home, which became the Florence Crittenden Home and later Steinway Hall.

Still other scenes showcase landmarks that are just memories today, such as the Flatiron Building at Main and Howard streets and the Empire House and the Buchtel, Windsor and Portage hotels.

The list goes on and on.

This Cuyahoga River scene is said by some to be where Commodore Perry built boats for the Battle of Lake Erie in the War of 1812.

This card, postmarked 1909, shows Smith Road before it was paved.

Akron in 1856, a view across the Pennsylvannia & Ohio Canal.

The Old Stone School built on South Broadway near Buchtel Avenue,
replaced a wooden building that dated to 1834.

This image of the Big Falls of Cuyahoga River prompted the sender in 1905 to conclude his message: "Fall-ow me and you'll wear diamonds."

In the Glen, crossing the Cuyahoga River by ferry, 1908.

An old scene along the Ohio & Erie Canal.

Lock 17 of the Ohio & Erie Canal.

Simon Perkins Jr., son of Akron founder Gen. Simon Perkins, and his wife, the former Grace Ingersoll Tod, moved into his Stone Mansion in 1837. It is now home to the Summit County Historical Society.

Abolitionist John Brown lived in this house, near the Perkins Stone Mansion, when he worked for Simon Perkins Jr.

The old Summit County Courthouse was completed in 1843.

The chapel at Glendale Cemetery is showcased in this view of its entrance.

Modern view of the University of Akron's Hower House, built by industrialist John H. Hower in 1871.

The Valley Railway station, West Market and Canal streets, was built in 1888.

Scene showing Union Park, a gift from the sons of Simon Perkins, and
Akron High School, prompted this message in 1909:
"Hello kid. This is where I took my morning bath. The gold fish are all dead now."

Grace Park, also a gift from Perkins' sons in the 1840s, was
named for Mrs. Simon Perkins Jr. Card was sent in 1909.

Neptune Park's fountain inspired the place to be renamed Fountain Park. The card was sent in 1910. The park is now named Alexander Park. The fountain is long gone, but a flower garden on the side facing west Market Street can be enjoyed each summer.

People traveled to Young's Hotel at Nesmith Lake by canoe on the Ohio & Erie Canal, as well as horse-drawn buggies long before era of automobiles. This card was postmarked 1911.

Howard and Market streets. Card was sent in 1907.

Looking north on Howard Street, which was incorrectly identified as "Harvard" in this card sent in 1909.

The old Masonic Temple at Howard and Mill streets is shown on a card sent in 1909, eight years before a new temple rose at Mill and High streets.

The Gothic Building and Colonial Theatre at Mill and High streets are showcased on this card, which was postmarked 1910.

The Northern Ohio railway bridge over the Ohio & Erie Canal was the subject of this card, which was sent in 1913, the year flood waters destroyed the canal.

This view of Howard Street looking up to North Hill was mailed in 1909, 13 years before the North Hill Viaduct spanned the Little Cuyahoga River and eased the trip from downtown.

West Hill, West Market Street looking west from the Everett Building over the roof top of the Empire House. The card was mailed in 1911; a year after the Empire House was demolished to make way for the Portage Hotel.

The Empire House, built in 1846-47, was Akron's finest
hotel in its day. The card was mailed in 1910.

Market Street looking west, past Empire House. Card was postmarked 1909.

The Everett Building, still at Main and Market streets, was built as the Academy of Music in 1871. To its left is the City Market House, built in 1905. Card was postmarked 1912.

Long view of Bowery-Howard-Main triangle. The Everett Building is visible down Main Street just over the back of the black buggy.

The Bowery-Howard-Main triangle showcased a wooden
building that predated the Flatiron Building.

The Flatiron Building, built in 1907, dominates the view looking north on Main Street.

The Collins buggy works is on the left in the foreground on Main Street looking west. The Whitelaw Building, which is still standing today next to the Civic Theatre, is across the street mid-block. Card was mailed in 1909.

Looking south on Main Street, the Unique Theatre is in the foreground. The Collins buggy works is also visible at far right. Card is postmarked 1915.

The northeast corner of Main and Mill streets, known as the Beacon Block, once housed predecessors of the Akron Beacon Journal. Card was mailed in 1912. *Courtesy of Leo Walter.*

The Buchtel Hotel, built in 1890 at the southeast corner of Main and Mill streets, was showcased in this card sent in 1909.

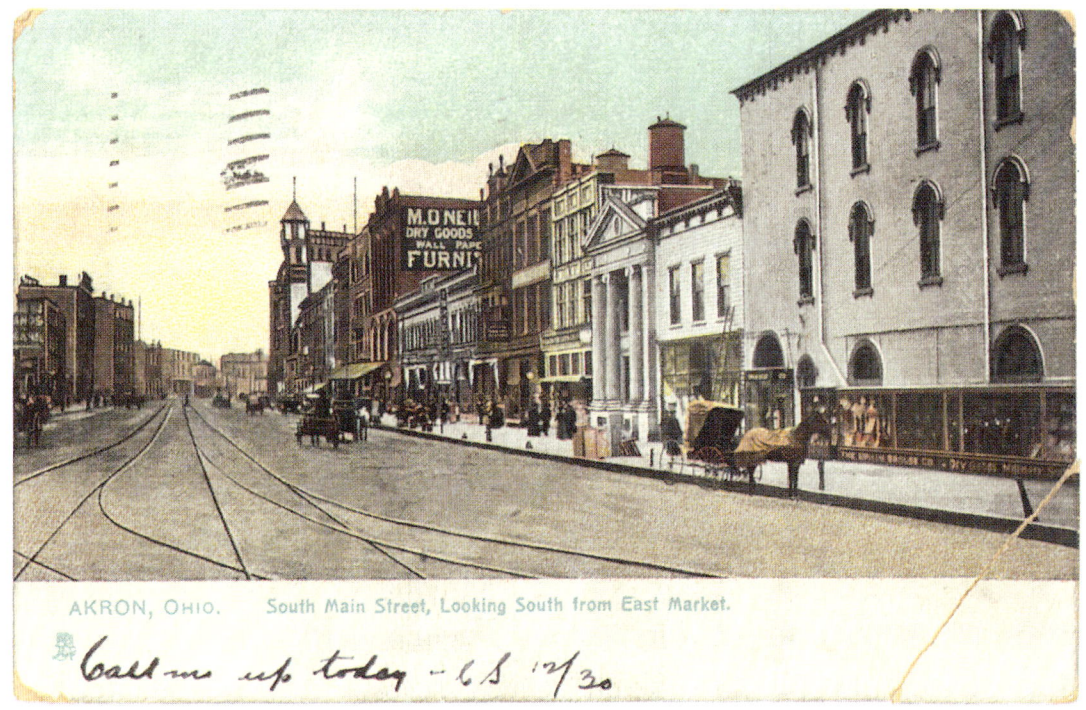

Main Street looking south from Market Street, circa 1905.

Union Depot was built in 1891 at College and Market for a town of 27,000 people and replaced in 1950 when Akron was 10 times larger.

The Mill Street Viaduct, beside what is now Quaker Square, after 1909.

The Windsor Hotel at Broadway and Mill Street. This was a temperance hotel owned by Ferdinand Schmacher, the "Cereal King." Card was sent in 1912.

The Akron Fire Department's Central Engine House at High and Church streets inspired this newsy message in 1909: "This department now has an auto-mobile hook & ladder." *Courtesy of Leo Walter.*

The old YMCA, built in 1904, stood on the site of the Mayflower Hotel, now the Mayflower Manor.

Summit County Jail beside the Courthouse. Card was postmarked 1907.

Peoples Savings Bank at Main and Exchange streets. Postmarked 1910.

The post office built in 1899, now the Akron Art Museum, was the subject of a card sent in 1924.

Greetings from Akron. Flowers were popular in the early period to convey pictures and messages.

33

Grace House, an early version of the YWCA, before 1910.

The interior of Grace House was the subject of this 1910 message: "This is where we hold forth in Akron. The walls are a lovely dark red and make the reception room most attractive."

Much enlarged Grace House, YWCA, later called
Sawan Building. Card postmarked 1914.

Summit County is spelled "Summet" on this card, which shows the Courthouse and, looking
south, St. Bernard's Catholic Church and the Jail. Inset is of the original Courthouse.

The German-American Music Hall was only three years old when this card was mailed in 1907. The Akron Beacon Journal now occupies the site. *Courtesy of Leo Walter.*

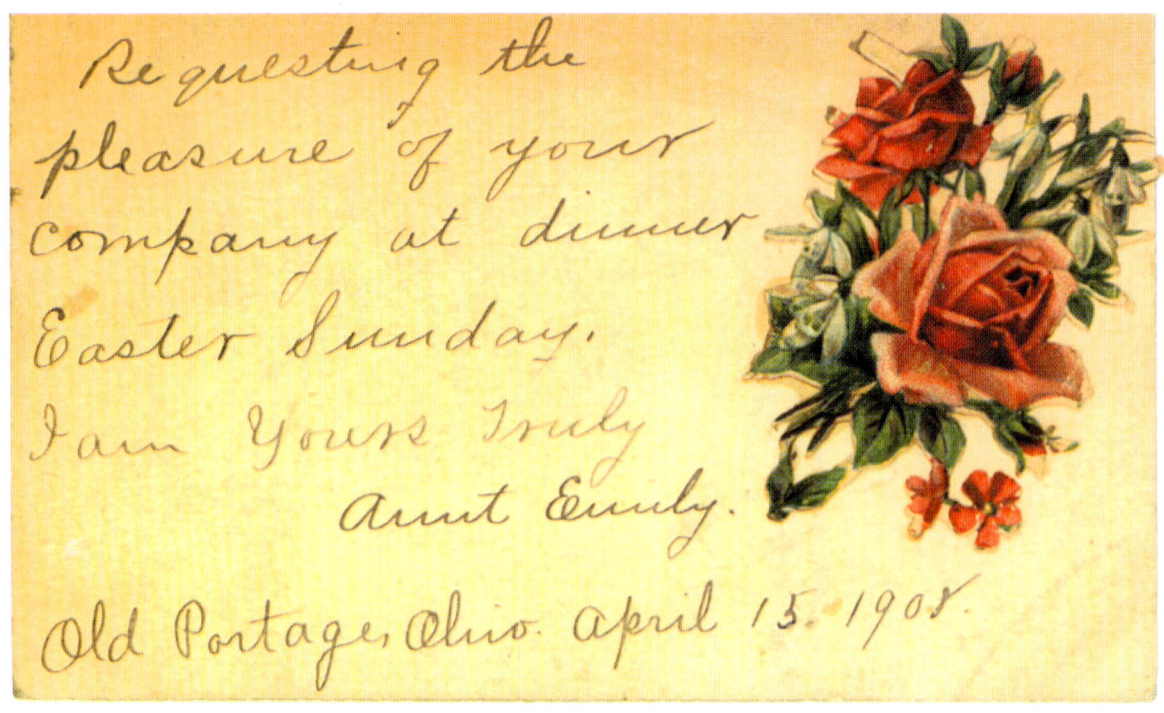

Old Portage, Ohio, at Merriman Road and Portage Path, was the return address on this card, mailed in 1908.

PORTAGE PATH MONUMENT, AKRON, OHIO

This Indian statue was erected in 1905 to mark where the Portage Path crossed West Market Street.

Close up of the Northern Ohio Traction & Light railroad bridge at the Gorge.

AKRON, OHIO. Lower and Higher Bridges over Cuyahoga River.

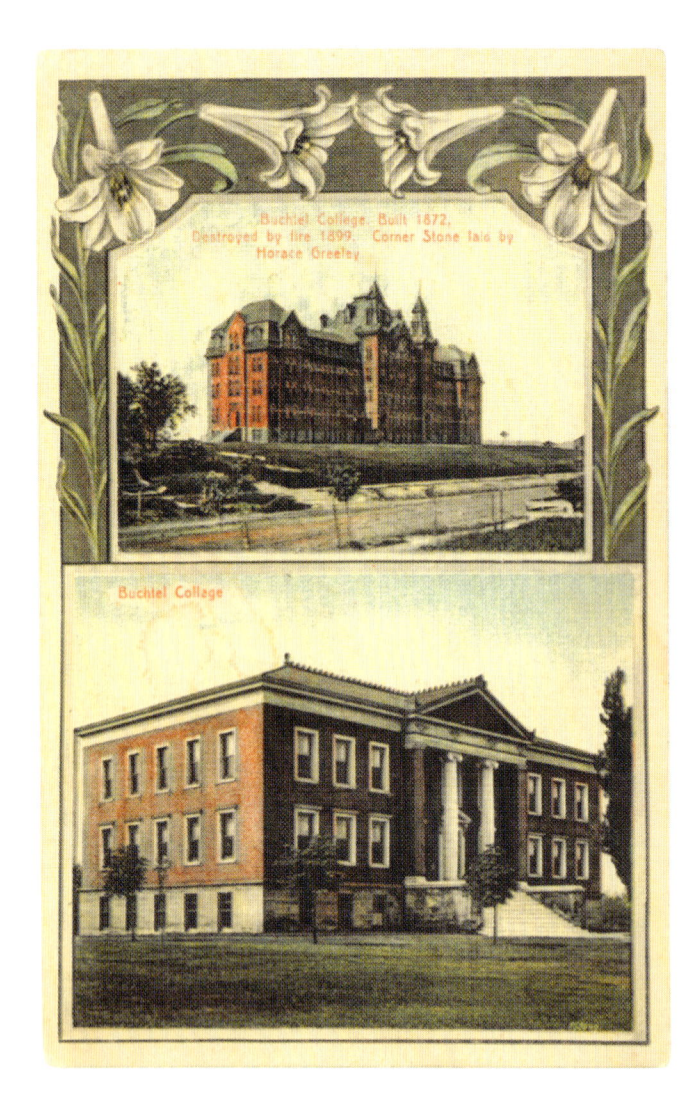

This card, mailed before 1910, shows both the original Buchtel College, which was completed in 1872 and burned down in 1899, and the new Buchtel Hall, built on the same site in 1901.

New Buchtel Hall, Crouse Gymnasium, the Academy (old Olin Hall) and Curtis Cottage. Postmarked 1909.

Robinson Clay Products, factory No. 9, early 1900s.

The Ohio & Erie Canal at Cascade Mills on Canal Street. The mills fronted on Howard Street and were known to later generations as the Quaker Oats Co.

This card, showing a canal boat at the Upper Basin behind B.F. Goodrich, bears a 1910 postmark.

This bird's-eye view of B.F. Goodrich and Diamond Rubber was mailed in 1909. *Courtesy of Agnes Barnett.*

The Diamond Rubber Co. tire-building department in this interior view, mailed in 1911. *Courtesy of Leo Walter.*

Goodyear offices and neighboring buildings in the early 1900s.

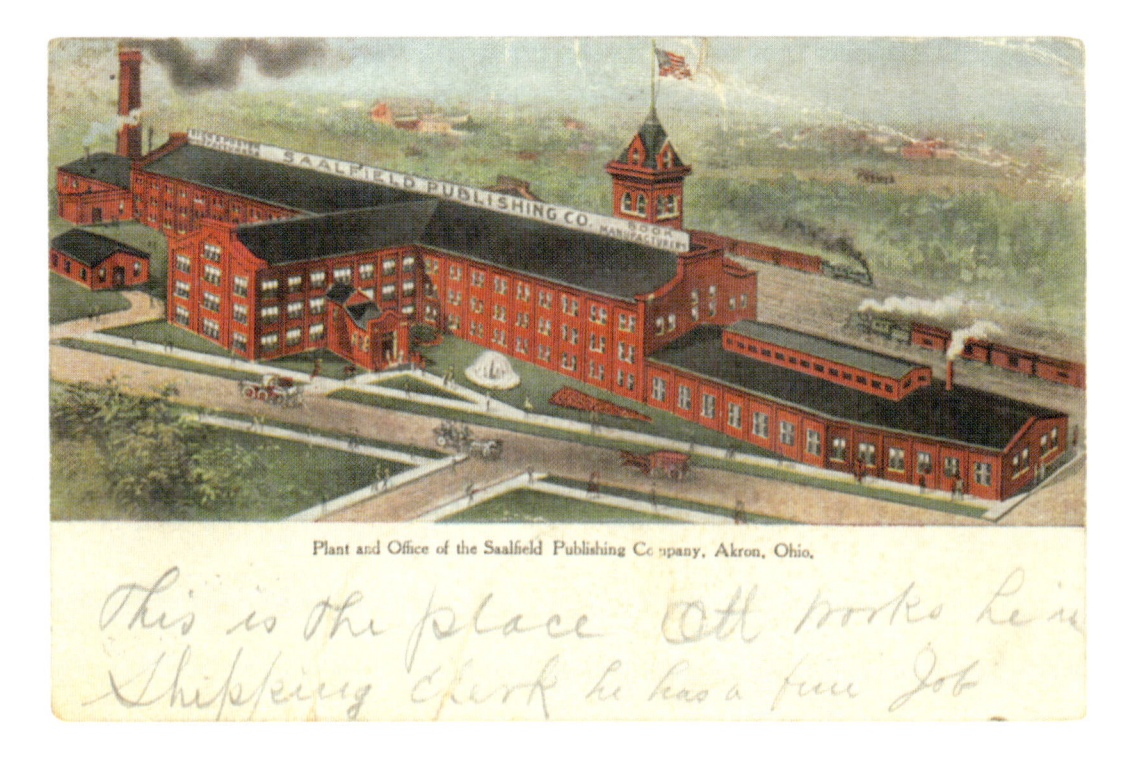

Saalfield Publishing Co. plant and office in South Akron, in the early 1900s.

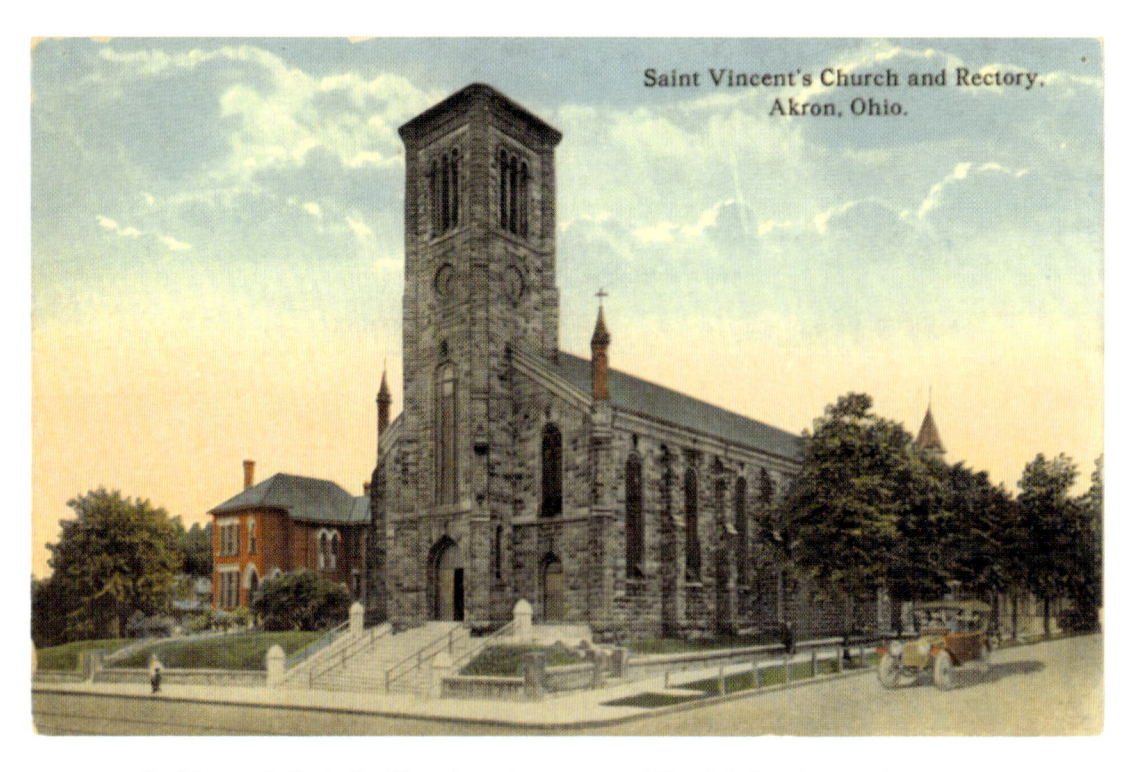

St. Vincent's Catholic Church and rectory on West Market Street, circa 1910.

Zion Luthern Church, still at High and East Bowery streets, was dedicated in 1877. *Courtesy of Jim Pahlau.*

First Baptist Church at Broadway, Mill and Market streets in early 1900s.

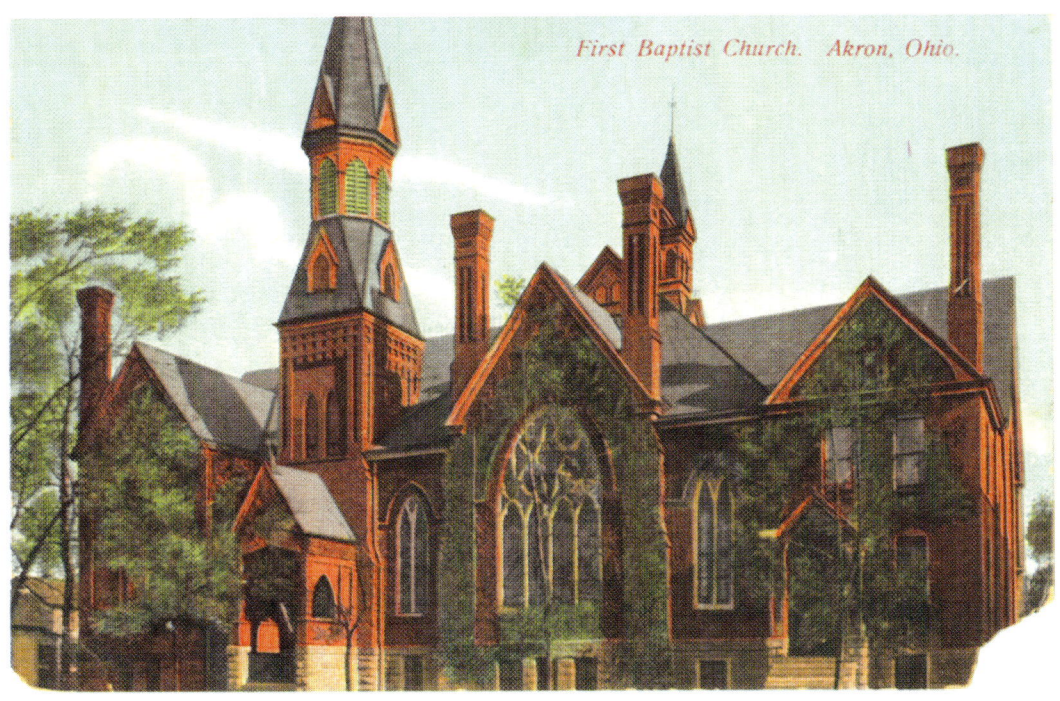

Woodland Methodist
Episcopal Church
in 1907.

Early 1900s view of the
Universalist
Church, which
was built in 1879
at Broadway
and Mill Street.

The First Methodist Episcopal Church's 1875 building at Broadway and Church Street, in 1909, two years before it burned down.

A 1907 view of St. Bernard's Catholic Church, completed in 1903, and the school on Broadway.

St. Paul's Episcopal Church's 1885 building (above) is now the University of Akron Ballet Center. Its adjacent 1909 building (below) is now
the University of Akron Firestone Conservatory.

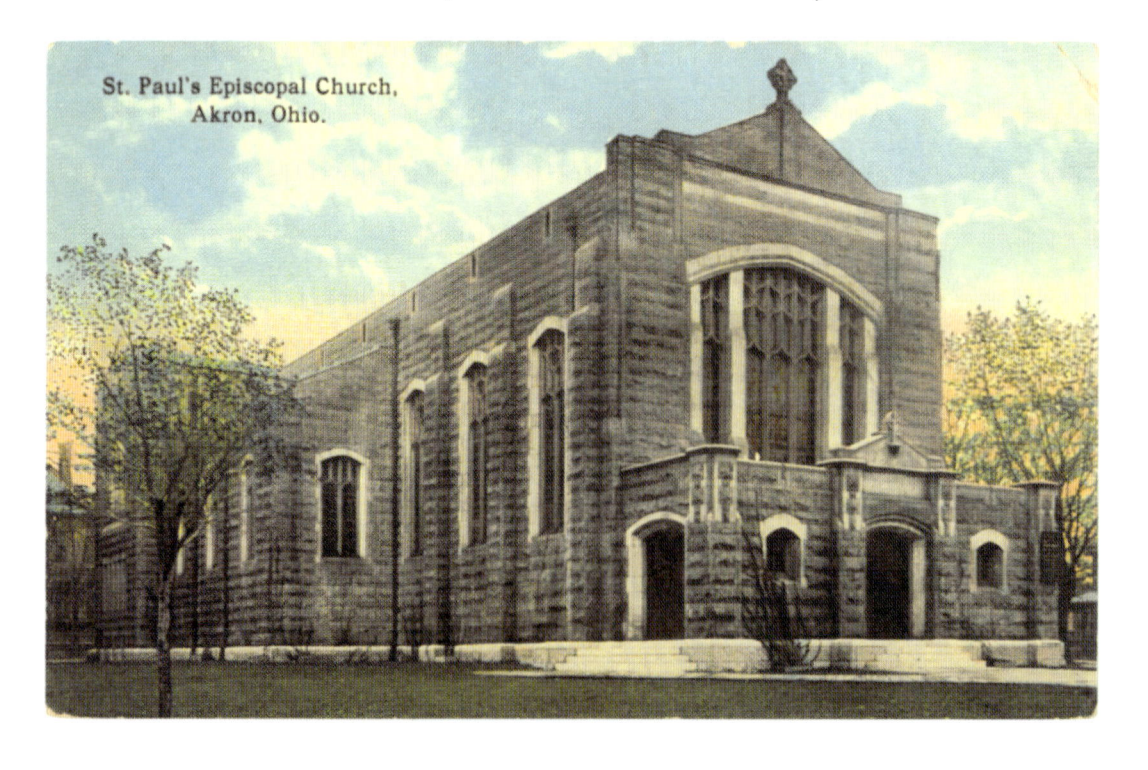

The First Congregational Church on South High Street as it looked in the late 1800s.

First Congregational Church. South High Street. Akron, Ohio.

The First Congregational Church's present building at Market and College streets was built in the early 1900s.

First Congregational Church, Akron, Ohio.

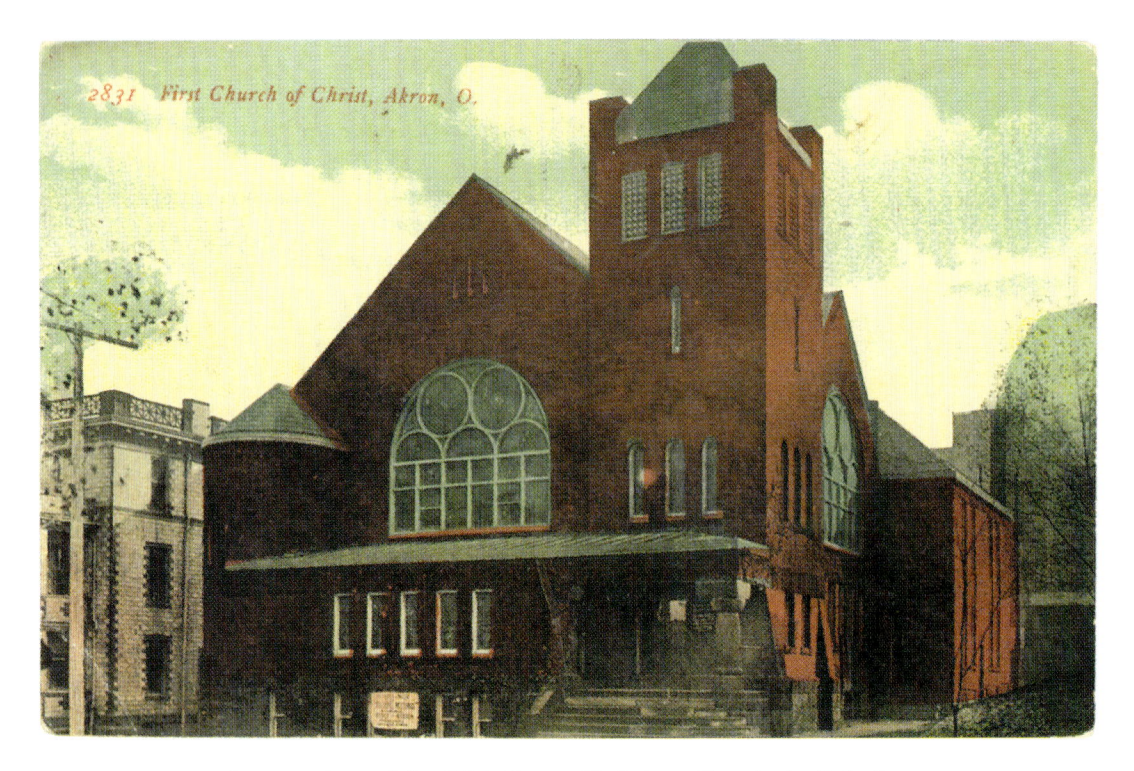

A 1911 view of the High Street Christian Church, built before turn of the century. Next door is the Garfield Hotel.

Card mailed in 1911 shows the Garfield Hotel on South High Street. Next door is part of the High Street Christian Church.

Grace School at Five Points was named for Grace Tod Perkins, Postmarked 1911.
In recent years the building was known as Schoolhouse Antiques.

Henry School behind City Hospital. It was built in 1883
and decommissioned in 1978. Postmarked 1912.

Perkins School, built 1872 at Bowery Street and West Exchange, is showcased on this card, postmarked 1913. An X on the card refers to the message on the back: "Here is the picture of the first school in which I taught in Akron. I stayed two weeks. It is the city normal school. The room in which I taught is the X."

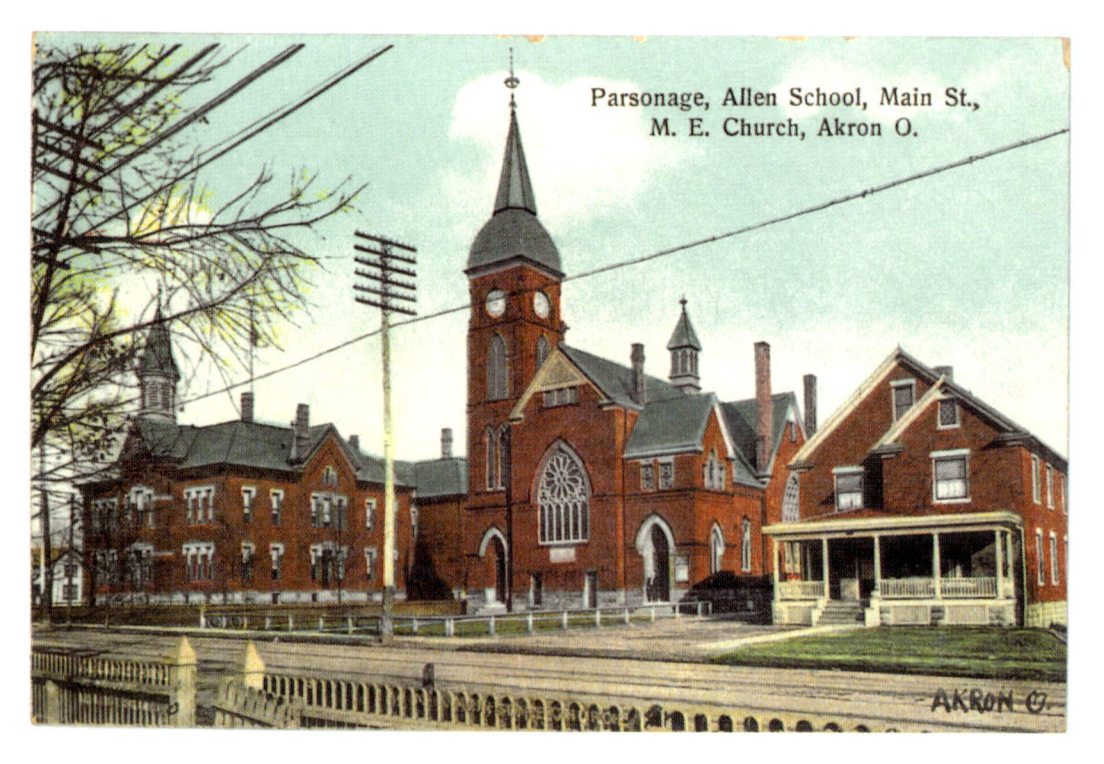

This card, sent in 1908, shows Allen School, which was built in 1879 and decommissioned in 1967, and the Methodist Episcopal Church and its Parsonage.

Kent School, built in 1891, on South Arlington Street, was decommissioned in 1940,

Findley School was built in 1906 at Tallmadge and Cuyahoga Falls avenues.

A 1911 view of Fraunfelter School, at Arlington Street and Buchtel Avenue. It later was the Hammel Business College and now is a branch of Oriana House.

Portage Path School, built 1908, was expanded twice, in 1916 and 1973.

A 1914 view of Senator Charles Dick's home at West Market Street and Marshall Avenue.
Its coach house was the first home of Weathervane Community Playhouse.

The Will Christy residence. Postmarked 1912.

Judge Jacob A. Kohler home on Market Street. Postmarked 1909.

Clara B. Ritchie home, built before 1900, was replaced by the Highland Towers. She was a descendant of Jonathan Hale and bequeathed Hale Homestead to the Western Reserve Historical Society.

This card, sent in 1909, shows the entrance to the B.G. Work residence at South Portage Path (misspelled as "Rath" on the card) and West Exchange Street. It now is home to the Akron Woman's City Club.

The Byron Robinson residence, built 1906, later became the Florence Crittenden Home and today is Steinway Hall.

A 1913 view of the P.E. Werner home. The fence and
wall surrounded the lot until September of 2000.

A 1911 view of Werner Press' factory and office building at Perkins and North Union streets.

The Mary Day Nursery was the located at Buchtel and High streets and was the forerunner of Children's Hospital Medical Center of Akron.

A 1919 view of City Hospital and its nurses' residence at East Market Street and Adolph Avenue includes the Bartges home where the hospital began in 1892.

The home of Mary and Charles Raymond, George T. Perkins' daughter and son-in-law, is now the site of the Akron Metropolitan Housing Authority's Saferstein Towers.

The Hower Building at West Market and Canal streets, which was used for storage and small manufacturing, was destroyed by fire on May 18, 1909.

1910 to the Great Depression

The boom that was Akron during the second decade of the 20th Century was heard and felt around the world as the rubber companies came into their own.

Goodyear, started in 1898 by brothers Frank A. and Charles W. Seiberling, was on its way to becoming the world's largest tire and rubber company.

Its competitors included Firestone, which entered the field in 1900; Goodrich, which merged with its neighbor, the Diamond Rubber Co., in 1912; General Tire & Rubber Co., which was started in 1915 by William O'Neil and Winfred E. Fouse; and smaller companies, among them Miller, Kelly-Springfield, Philadelphia, Swinehart Tire & Rubber, Faultless Rubber, Motz Clincher Tire & Rubber, Stein Double Cushion Tire and Union Rubber.

The growing auto industry and the production demands of World War I resulted in companies importing so many workers that Akron became the fastest growing city in the world. Its population, which was 69,000 in 1910, soared to more than 208,000 by 1920.

Housing was in such short supply that rooming house dwellers slept in shifts and families lived in attics, basements, garages, converted chicken coops and in shanties.

Postcards and their messages from this period reflected the mood of the times. Some examples:

"Am seeing the sights in Akron. This is no place for a minister's son."

"I think you could get work now anytime."

"Here at last. No permanent add(ress). Yet may move out to a Suburb, as this is a dirty, hot town."

Industrialists got away from the soot and smoke by building their homes on Akron's west side. Frank A. Seiberling and Harvey S. Firestone were among them, but they also built two neighborhoods, Goodyear Heights and Firestone Park, to meet their employees' housing needs.

Postcards in this section feature many examples of Akron's phenomenal residential development for both the elite and the masses. Examples of the former include Seiberling's Stan Hywet Hall, built in 1915 and today a community foundation-operated museum, and Firestone's Harbel Manor, which dated to the same period and was razed in 1959.

Other cards chronicle the growth of Akron's skyline, focus on where its residents went to school, shopped, gathered to worship and enjoyed recreation, and showcase the enormous Airdock, built by the Goodyear Zeppelin Corp. on the eve of the Great Depression in 1929.

This undated card speaks volumes about the boom times: "Am seeing the sights in Akron. This is no place for a minister's son."

A parade headed south in this 1910 view of South Main Street.

A 1918 view of Main Street looking south, showcases the
B.F. Goodrich and Diamond Rubber companies.

Bird's-eye view of Main Street looking north, circa 1920.

B.F. Goodrich Co. called itself "largest in the world" in 1910 when this was postmarked.

Looking west at the B.F. Goodrich works in the early days.

The Diamond Rubber, shown in card postmarked 1913, merged with B.F. Goodrich in 1912. *Courtesy of Leo Walter.*

This card showcased the Diamond Band. Its message in 1912: "I think you could get work now anytime." *Courtesy of Leo Walter*

63

The Goodyear Tire & Rubber Co. advertised its carriage tire department in this card, postmarked 1911. The message: "What do you need in Rubber Carriage Tires? Look up your stock. Send us your orders now, and have the best on earth. Goodyear Tire and Rubber Co., Akron, O."

Quitting time at Goodyear. The card was sent in 1917.

A Goodyear Heights promotional card focused on housing and education the company-developed neighborhood offered.

Bingham Path-Goodyear Avenue triangle park in Goodyear Heights, circa 1915.

The message on this Firestone Tire & Rubber Co. card, sent in 1912, was: "Had the pleasure of going thru the Firestone factory today. Am more enthusiastic than ever over their tires."

General Tire & Rubber Co. was started on East Market Street in 1915. *Courtesy of Leo Walter.*

A 1920s view of Mohawk Rubber Co.

This Kelly-Springfield Tire Co. card was mailed in 1915

This Star Rubber Co. card was mailed in 1912. *Courtesy of Leo Walter.*

A card sent in 1916 showcases the Philadelphia Rubber Works' Akron reclaiming plant.

This view of the Quaker Oats Co. Howard Street plant, looking north, was mailed in 1917, four years after it was built.

Quaker Oats' Howard Street plant, looking south.

The Great Western Cereal Co., shown in this 1915 postmarked card, was part of the Quaker Oats Co.

This view of the Quaker Oats complex on Mill Street was mailed in 1915.

Central Savings & Trust Co., Hamilton Building, at Mill and
Main streets, now site of the First National Tower.

This view of the Akron Savings & Loan Building, Bowery and
South Main streets at Howard Street, was sent in 1914.

HOTEL PORTAGE, AKRON, OHIO.

The Portage Hotel, built in 1912 at Main and Market streets, was Akron's leading hotel until the Art Deco-styled Mayflower Hotel was built in 1931.

HOTEL HOWE, AKRON, OHIO.

The Hotel Howe, built 1915 on the site of Pingree's livery stable, was three years old when this card was mailed.

The Hotel Marne, South Main Street just south of State Street, circa 1920.

HOTEL MARNE, AKRON, OHIO.

The Hotel Akron was built at East Market Street and Broadway during the boom.

Hotel Akron, Akron, Ohio

EAST MARKET STREET FROM HOTEL PORTAGE, AKRON

This view of East Market Street as seen from the Portage Hotel was sent in 1917.

10.

The Strand Theatre on South Main Street north of Bowery Street
was two years old when this card was mailed in 1917.

The Ohio Building, now the Summit County office building, was new
when this card was sent in 1916. Two more stories were added later.

MASONIC TEMPLE, AKRON, OHIO.

The Masonic Temple was built at Mill and High streets in 1917.

The Ohio National Guard Armory on South High Street, now site of Ocasek State Office Building, was completed in 1918.

ARMORY, O. N. G., AKRON, OHIO.

Terminal Building, Akron, Ohio.

The Terminal Building, shown around 1930, was built as the Northern Ohio Traction and Light building and car barns. With two stories added, it later was home to Ohio Edison and today houses the Summit County Department of Human Services.

METROPOLITAN BUILDING, AKRON, OHIO.

The Metropolitan Building was built in 1918 on the former site of the Doyle lumberyard on Main Street.

The United Building was built in 1922 at East Market and South Main streets.

UNITED BUILDING, AKRON, OHIO   B-739

The U.S. Post Office completed in 1928 at East Market and Prospect streets, is now the Charles Mayer Studios.

THE NEW POST OFFICE, AKRON, OHIO   123255

This view of the Elks Temple on North High Street was mailed in 1916, the year it was built. The site was previously occupied by a Jewish temple and, before that, St. Paul's Episcopal Church.

This view of the Medford Building, home of Actual Business College, was sent in 1916. At its left was the Salvation Army Citadel on North Main Street.

The Central Garage on Ash Street, shown in a card sent in 1921, had room for 5,000 cars.

This view of National City Bank, on South Main Street between East Exchange Street and today's site of Canal Park, was mailed in 1917.

MAIN STREET, LOOKING NORTH FROM EXCHANGE STREET, AKRON, OHIO.

This view of Main Street, looking north from East Exchange, features the Bond Hotel on west the side and the Marne Hotel on the east. It was mailed in 1926. The Bond, where writer Hart Crane lived in Akron, later was the Anthony Wayne Hotel.

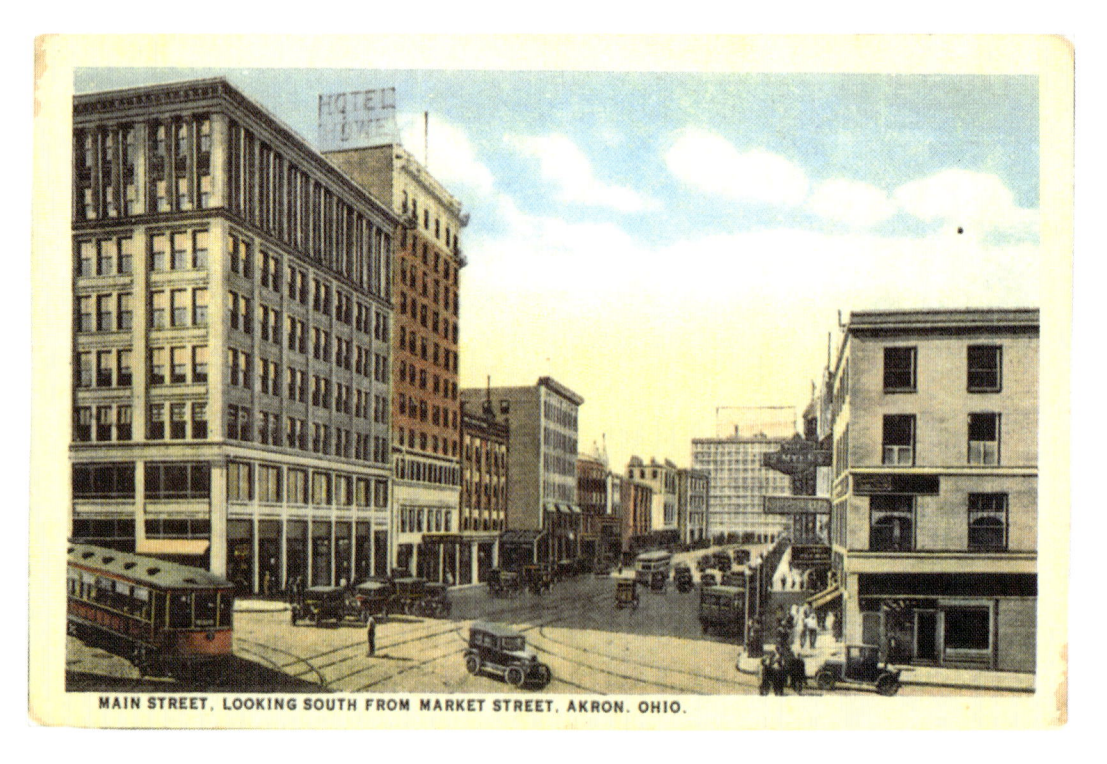

MAIN STREET, LOOKING SOUTH FROM MARKET STREET, AKRON, OHIO.

A view of Main Street looking south from Market Street, circa 1930. The United Building is on the left hand corner, the Howe Hotel is next to it.

This card, mailed in 1919, shows the M. O'Neil Co. when it was between East Market and Mill streets on South Main.

M. O'Neil Co. department store, built in 1928 at South Main and State streets, today is the home of a law firm. The card was postmarked 1946.

C.H. Yeager Co. department store, partly in the former O'Neil's and Polsky's buildings, circa 1930.

The message on this card, featuring the Fire Department, City Hall and First Second National Bank building, and mailed to Salem, Ohio, in 1915, was in German.

The Municipal Building
was built in 1926 at
High and Church streets.

This card, showcasing the
Police Station, Municipal
Building and First Trust &
Savings Bank on High Street,
bore a less than flattering
message: "Here at last.
No permanent add(ress).
Yet may move out to a
Suburb, as this is a
dirty, hot town."

MUNICIPAL BUILDING, AKRON, OHIO.

POLICE STATION, MUNICIPAL BUILDING AND FIRST TRUST AND SAVINGS BANK, AKRON, OHIO.

The John Brown
Monument, created
from a column from the
original Summit County
Court House, stands
in Perkins Park. The
card was sent in 1912.

The North Hill Viaduct,
which carried Main
Street over the Little
Cuyahoga River valley,
circa 1930.

Perkins Square Playground, established by playground advocate
Margaret Barnhardt. Card was postmarked 1916.

Perkins Park spring, largely paid for by school children in honor of Margaret Barnhardt.

New dam at the Cuyahoga River Gorge, completed in 1914.

Northern Ohio Traction & Light Co. powerhouse and trolley bridge over the Cuyahoga River. Card was sent in 1919.

Aerial view of the old High Level Bridge between Akron and Cuyahoga Falls.

East Market Gardens, a popular place for dancing, was next to
the Congregational Church on East Market Street.

Parking lot at entrance to Summit Beach Park.
Card was sent in 1921. *Courtesy of Leo Walter.*

The Glenn Curtiss Hydro-Aeroplane landed at Summit Lake.
Sent in 1918. *Courtesy of Leo Walter.*

Hilarity Hall, the House of Fun, Summit Beach Park, 1927. *Courtesy of Leo Walter.*

Summit Beach Park dance hall and roller rink.   Mailed in 1923.

Summit County Fair grandstands at Old Forge Field. *Courtesy of Leo Walter.*

It was standing room only at League Park, Beaver and Excelsior streets, and everyone dressed for the game. *Courtesy of Leo Walter.*

Buchtel Avenue and East Market Street. Mailed in 1912.

East Market Street and Case Avenue, later site of Wagon Wheel Cafe.

Portage County Club, started as a six-hole course at Perkins Hill, moved to the former Doyle farm, Portage Path at Twin Oaks Road, in 1905. The card was mailed in 1912.

Dodge Avenue and Portage Path. Sent in 1914.

Summit County Infirmary, now site of Westminster Presbyterian Church. The Infirmary was built in 1864 on land first purchased by Summit County in 1849 for the poor. It became a farm of about 230 acres. Mailed in 1914.

People's Hospital, now Akron General Medical Center, was two years old when this card was mailed in 1916.

Summit County Children's Home on South Arlington Street. Postmarked in 1917.

The Northern Ohio Traction and Light car barns at South Main Street and Miller Avenue were used until 1912. *Courtesy of Leo Walter.*

South Main Street and Miller Avenue.

The Firestone Park Trust & Savings Bank - later Firestone Bank -
was at Miller Avenue and South Main Street.

West Congregational Church, Akron, Ohio.

West Congregational Church, built during the last half of 19th Century at West Market and Balch streets, is now the site of the Red Cross Building. Card's 1911 message asks friend to phone and gives two numbers, one of each of Akron's telephone companies.

This card, mailed in 1915, showcases the First Methodist Episcopal Church on Mill Street, which was built to replace the one that burned down in 1911. It was destroyed by fire in 1994 and replaced by a new structure on the same location.

FIRST M. E. CHURCH, AKRON, OHIO.

This card was mailed in 1914, two years after Temple Israel
was built on Merriman Road at Marshall Avenue.

Annunciation Catholic Church on Kent Street off
East Market Street was dedicated in 1913.

The Evangelical Lutheran Church of the Holy Trinity, Akron, Ohio.

This was sent in 1917, three years after the Evangelical Lutheran Church of the Holy Trinity was built facing Grace Park on Prospect Street.

St. Mary's Catholic Church was built in 1916 at West Thornton and Coburn streets.

SAINT MARY'S CATHOLIC CHURCH, AKRON, OHIO.

Grace Reformed Church, State and Bowery streets. *Courtesy of Leo Walter.*

Church of Our Saviour, Balch and Crosby streets. Mailed in 1917.

St. John's Evangelical Lutheran Church.

First Church of Christ, Scientist. Postmarked 1917. The Fir Hill location became part of the Chapel on Fir Hill when First Church moved to a new building.

F. A. SIEBERLING RESIDENCE AND GARDENS, AKRON, OHIO.

Stan Hywet, built in 1915 by F.A. Seiberling, has been a community foundation-operated museum since the late 1950s. Postmarked 1921.

10844. H. A. Galt Residence, Akron, Ohio

Industrialist Hugh A. Galt's residence on West Market Street has had a variety of institutional uses in later years. The card was mailed to Switzerland in 1913 for 2 cents postage.

The Arthur H. Marks residence on West Market Street became
Our Lady of the Elms convent and school. Card was mailed in 1915.

This card was mailed in 1912, five years after F.H. Adams built the home he called
Rockynol, now the site of Rockynol retirement community on West Market Street.

Garden view at Harbel Manor. Sarah's 1931 message to Blanche in Mowersville, Pa.: "Keep this postcard and show it to Dad because this is where the Firestone residence is." *Courtesy of Leo Walter.*

The Sumner Home on Merriman Road, opened in 1951 in the former Harvey H. and Eleanor Gibbs residence.

South High School at Main and Thorton streets, was a year old when this was sent in 1912. It later became Thorton Junior High and was used until 1979.

West High School, built in 1913 on Maple Street at Balch Street, is now the privately-owned West High Apartments.

East High School, now Goodyear Middle School, was built in 1918.

Perkins School, across from Perkins Square, later became
Hower Trade School. Card was mailed in 1924.

1930 to 1950

Just as World War I fueled Akron's unprecedented growth in the years leading up to 1920, World War II pulled the city out of the Great Depression.

But the difficult years at the beginning of the Depression were a time in which Akron saw the construction of its first skyscraper, the 26-story First National Tower, and two other landmarks, a new YMCA and the Mayflower Hotel (now the Mayflower Manor apartments).

Polsky's opened its new department store (now part of the University of Akron) across from O'Neil's department store in 1930. The Ohio Bell Telephone building (now Ameritech) and North High School were opened in 1931.

The era also saw the emergence of the United Rubber Workers union, which was born in 1936 and won recognition after a strike that year against Goodyear.

The Akron-Fulton municipal airport grew during the 1930s, beginning with the construction of an administration building (now a restaurant).

The Akron Rubber Bowl, built adjacent to the airport and dedicated - twice - on Aug. 10, 1940 and a year later, on Aug. 16, was just one of a host of WPA projects that helped thousands of unemployed workers survive the Depression.

Other projects included construction or improvement of 46 playgrounds, 133 bridges and 600 miles of streets and roads around Summit County.

Another breakthrough of the period was the creation in 1938 of the Akron Metropolitan Housing Authority, which began its 60-year effort to provide decent homes for low-income families with the construction of the Elizabeth Park Homes just north of downtown.

By 1940 Akron industry was geared for war. Goodyear, Firestone and General Tire were building gas masks and Firestone began building an anti-aircraft gun for use in Great Britain. Goodyear Zeppelin, which became the Goodyear Aircraft Corp., began producing military plane tail assemblies and went on to build 3,700 Corsair fighters, more than 150 lighter-than-air craft for the Navy, and 100,000 parts for 10 other types of fighter planes and bombers.

It was the construction industry's turn to thrive when the war ended and with it building restrictions that had made it difficult to meet the demand for housing. As new homes went up at a feverish pace, Akron also experienced a surge in the construction of new churches.

Another boom was beginning.

A contemporary view of the Akron Civic Theatre,
which was built as Loew's Theatre in 1929.

The A. Polsky department store, built in 1930 at South Main
and State streets, today is part of the University of Akron.

The Mayflower Hotel, now the Mayflower Manor apartments, was new when this card was mailed in 1932.

The YMCA was built in 1931.

North High School was built in 1931 on Gorge Boulevard.

The Ohio Bell Telephone building, now Ameritech, was built in 1932 on Bowery Street. The Central Garage is in the background.

The Akron Municipal Airport terminal is now a restaurant.

A 1931 view of the Goodyear Zeppelin Corp. Airdock, with doors partially opened. Built in 1929, the blimp and dirigible hangar and factory evolved into Goodyear Aircraft Corp. and Goodyear Aerospace before being sold to Loral in 1987. Lockheed Martin has owned it since 1996.

The U.S. Navy dirigible Akron flies over Goodyear plants
1 and 2, the Goodyear Bank and Goodyear Hall.

This card, showcasing Akron's skyline from Summit Lake, was mailed in 1948.

801—First National Tower, Akron, Ohio

Home of Greater Akron's only National Bank

The First National Tower, completed 1932 at South Main and Mill streets, today is home to First Merit Bank.

First Central Trust, soon to become the First National Bank, in 1932.

MAIN BANKING LOBBY, THE CENTRAL DEPOSITORS BANK & TRUST COMPANY

Main Street looking north from West Buchtel Avenue, circa 1940.

A 1950s view of Main Street looking north from West Buchtel Avenue.

An aerial view of South Main Street looking south, circa 1950.

South Main Street looking north from the Flatiron Building, circa 1940.

Bird's-eye view of First Central Trust Building, circa 1930.

Garden Grille, a leading Akron restaurant, on South Main
Street, across from Loew's Theatre, circa 1940.

Postwar aerial view of Goodyear's Airdock.

The Goodyear Research Building.

Greetings from Akron showing some art deco structures.

A rubber tire frames the Goodyear, Firestone and
B.F. Goodrich companies in this card, circa 1950.

1950 to Present

This final section begins and ends with aerial views of the University of Akron. One is from the 1950s. The other looks to the future, as a Goodyear blimp soars over the university's $17 million Goodyear Polymer Science Center.

The Center houses four university polymer divisions, which hit the ground running with research grants and government and corporate contracts when its doors opened in 1990.

The University's growth, from a Universalist Church-sponsored college in 1870 to a municipal institution in 1913 to a state university in 1967, mirrors the growth of Akron. The University stretched from its original hilltop campus to Main Street with its acquisition of the Polsky Building in the 1990s.

Postcards in this section showcase many other examples of Akron's skill at adaptive reuse of its buildings, beginning with its old libraries and post offices.

The Akron Art Institute was born in the basement of the Carnegie Library, which was featured on the 1905 card at the beginning of this book. When the Institute became the Akron Art Museum, it moved across East Market Street to an Italianate building that first saw life as the main post office in 1899, and a law firm remodeled and took over the former library.

The game of musical offices continued into the 1990s, when the law firm bought and remodeled the former O'Neil's department store building for its headquarters and the City of Akron bought the former Carnegie Library.

The Charles Mayer Studios have been headquartered at East Market and Prospect streets for so long that many people don't realize the building also began as a latter day main post office.

Quaker Square, featuring shops and a Hilton Hotel in the former Quaker Oats Co. silos and adjoining buildings, was a 1970s example of these urban and industrial transformations.

The B.F. Goodrich complex, where the rubber industry began in 1870, is now Canal Place at its southern end and, in the renovated north end, headquarters of the Advanced Elastomer Systems, a polymer company that moved to Akron from St. Louis.

Postcards in this section also reflect the growth in size and scope of Akron's hospitals during the second half of the 20th Century and showcase the buildings that are symbolic of its place in the 21st Century, such as Inventure Place, home of the National Inventors Hall of Fame; Canal Park stadium, home of the Akron Aeros; and the John S. Knight Convention Center.

A 1950s aerial view of the University of Akron.

Early view the University Club, now the University
of Akron's Martin University Center.

The Harvey S. Firestone statue near Main Street and Firestone Parkway was dedicated in 1950.

A 1950s view of the Akron Art Institute's first home, the former Carnegie Library. The building later was home to a law firm.

Union Depot soon after it was completed in 1950. It now is the University of Akron's Buckingham Building and home to the Pan African Culture and Research Center.

1950s view of the Greyhound Bus Terminal, now the site of the University of Akron College of Business Administration.

Original home of the Akron Baptist Temple, dedicated in 1937.

Contemporary view of the Akron Baptist Temple.

Our Lady of the Elms' elementary school gymnasium was originally the high school.

Aerial view of the Chapel on Fir Hill.

Mid-20th Century view of Children's Hospital Medical Center of Akron, which began as the Mary Day Nursery.

Mid-20th Century view of Akron City Hospital, now part of the Summa Health System.

A 1960s view of Akron General Hospital, which began as People's Hospital and now is called Akron General Medical Center.

Aerial view of Akron General Medical Center in the 1990s.

Mid-20th Century view of Derby Downs, home of the All-American Soap Box Derby.

The Akron Rubber Bowl, built 1939 by WPA workers,
is now owned by the University of Akron.

The Goodyear tire assembly line in the 1960s.

Cascade Plaza in the middle of downtown, circa 1970.
Courtesy of Agnes Barnett.

The City-County Safety Building (to the right of the Summit County Courthouse) was new when this view was captured in the late 1960s.

Contemporary view of the Akron-Summit County Library on South Main Street.

Quaker Square today and in 1944, when the Quaker Oats Co. was in operation there.

The University of Akron's E.J. Thomas Performing Arts Hall opened in 1973.

The Akron Art Museum and sculpture garden, circa 1990.

This Akron-Summit County Convention and Visitor Bureau card showcases Inventure Place, the John S. Knight Convention Center, the Cuyahoga Valley Scenic Railroad train in Cuyahoga Valley National Recreation Area and Akron's skyline.

Lock 2 Park, behind Canal Park stadium, circa 1990.

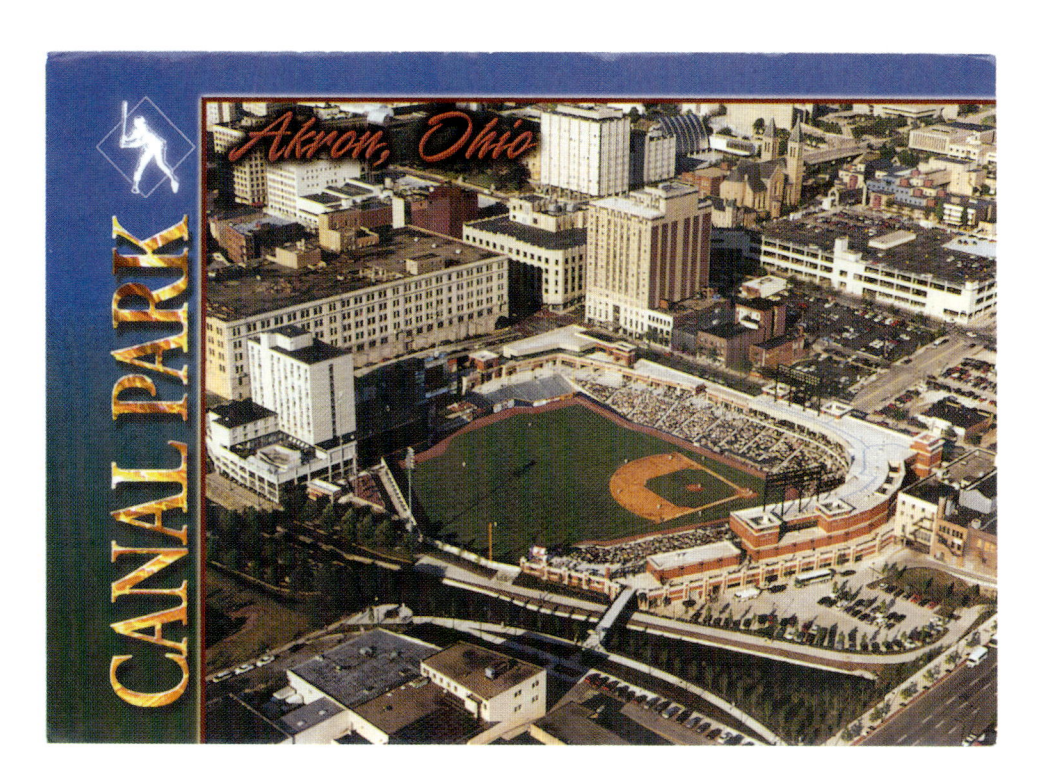

Canal Park stadium, home of the Akron Aeros, opened in 1997.

Glendale Cemetery is in the foreground of this aerial view of
downtown Akron from west of the Innerbelt.

Contemporary view of the Old Stone School, with
the University of Akron in the background.

The Spirit of Akron sails above the University of Akron's $17 million Goodyear Polymer Science Center, which opened in 1990.